Whether You Like It or Not

(A Collection of Poetry, Notes, and Short Stories)

Brooke "Alex" Davis

"Art has to be a kind of confession. I don't mean a true confession in the sense of that dreary magazine. The effort, it seems to me, is: if you can examine and face your life, you can discover the terms with which you are connected to other lives, and they can discover, too, the terms with which they are connected to other people."

James Baldwin

● ● ●

Introduction

In this book you will find various poems, short stories, and notes that I wrote over the past few years while voyaging through my second-wind of motherhood and my first attempt at a Bachelor's Degree (2016-2021). While these works were written in this specific time frame, they all encompass different parts of my life from childhood to now.

There is no central theme of love or self-discovery, only a representation of the non-linear journey of life thus far. Single motherhood, grief, self-deprivation, lonliness, happiness, depression, and well-earned, well-deserved success are all topics explored through prose, poetry, and jotted-down notes.

The phrase 'whether you like it or not' is a reoccuring theme in my life in that many of the things I experience are happening whether I like it or not. In our life's journey there are times when we will have to face the painful, the uncomfortable, the difficult; these feelings and emotions have to be faced head on whether we like it or not, because honestly, who likes it? It has to be done in order to heal, in order to move forward, in order to *learn and unlearn.*

While my writing is indeed therapeutic for myself, I find that sharing it helps me more because in doing so, others can see they are not alone. So often we go through life assuming that our troubles are isolated only to us and that so many would not understand, when in reality it's quite the opposite. There are troves of readers who turn to literature to seek out that relation to others in order to feel seen.

I see you.

I feel you.

I hope you see and feel me, too.

Lonliness

This space is empty and vast;

Although I try to run, it's inescapable.

These seasons they seem to last;

It's everywhere I am, it's palpable.

Everyone is here, yet everyone is gone;

I'm surrounded and I'm deserted.

Like a southern mosquito it feeds on

everything that leaves us disconcerted.

This space is empty & vast;
Although I try to run,
it's inescapable.
These seasons they seem to last;
It's everywhere I am, it's
palpable.

Everyone is here, yet everyone is
gone;
I'm surrounded & I'm deserted.
Like a southern mosquito
it feeds on
everything that leaves us
disconcerted.

Overwhelming Feeling

There is this overwhelming feeling –

it taunts me

everyday.

Still unsure of what it is,

but sure

it won't go away.

It wants me to acknowledge it,

and make it come to life –

but I know once I start

unpacking shit

this overwhelming feeling

won't be packing light.

● ● ●

June 20, 2018

There is this overwhelming
feeling.
It taunts me everyday.
Still unsure of what it is
But sure it won't go away.
It wants me to acknowledge it
and make it come to life
But, I know once I start
unpacking shit,
This overwhelming feeling
won't be packing light...

September 25, 1999

The day after my Mom died, me and my sister were told to stick little circle neon-colored tags onto items in our rooms, the living room, and kitchen. I didn't know it then, but my Aunt Valerie was eager to sell everything there was to sell to get a return on the funeral she had to pay for. I didn't want to get rid of my Nintendo 64 or my toy box full of toys, but I didn't have a choice. And Mom wasn't there to stick up for me. I slowly began to figure out that she wasn't coming back. Just days after she passed, I was never the same again.

The day of, I remember my mom being sick. She was technically always sick, seeing that she was diagnosed with head and neck cancer when I was in the second grade. I suppose they caught the cancer later than anyone would have hoped and so she had to have surgery right away. She had a laryngectomy, which is the removal of your voice-box, and also had her tongue removed. The day she came home from surgery she was a completely different person. She could no longer eat food, instead having to poor cans of vanilla Ensure into a feeding tube surgically inserted in her stomach. With no tongue, she could no longer swallow, and instead used a suction machine – like a dentist suction wand – every time she needed to swallow. Her chin would stay permanently swollen and when I would sit in her lap, I would trace my finger on the trail of her staple scars – behind her ear, down her neck, across her shoulder blade. Every day she was sick. Her coughs would permeate through the hallway and into mine and my sister's bedroom, and to this day I can't bear to hear a sick person's cough. But on the day of, she was a different type of sick.

That morning my mom wasn't feeling well. My Aunt Erika came over to pick me up and take me to the mall. My mom knew how much I loved music and instructed my aunt to take me to the mall to pick out a CD, just like me and her used to. When me, my mom, and my sister lived in Oceano, she would take me to Boo's Record Store twenty minutes away in San Luis Obispo to pick out a cassette tape. I was always only allowed to get one at a time. On the wall in the shop, they would have the cassette singles lined on a shelf according to what was popular or on the charts at the time. One day I went home with TLC's "Diggin' on You," -- surprisingly I favored this song over Waterfalls – and another time I convinced my mom to buy me Coolio's "Gangsta's Paradise." On this day, my aunt took me to a Sam Goody in the mall in Athens, Georgia. CD's were more popular at this time in 1999, so I went with the CD single of LFO's "Summer Girls." I first heard it on MTV. To this day, I won't listen to the song.

When me and my Aunt Erika arrived back at my house, more family members were there – my Aunt Jacquelyn, my mom's mom, "Grams" and my aunt's husbands. As an eleven-year-old, I didn't think much of it and headed to my room to listen to my new CD in the portable boombox I got for Christmas the year before. '*I like girls that wear Abercrombie and Fitch, I'd take her if I* had one wish, but she's been gone since that summer, that summer.' The song was undoubtedly catchy. This was during the Britney Spears, "Hit Me Baby One More Time" era. After listening through the song a couple of times, my Grams came to my bedroom door and told me to come in the living room. When I reached the end of the hallway, I noticed that everyone was in the living room, even my sister. I sat criss-cross-applesauce on the carpet near the edge of my mom's blue recliner. Adults were talking amongst one another and huddled around my mom. I asked what was going on, and Grams said, "Your mom is going to sleep for a while."

Going to sleep for a while? This confused me so I asked another question, "She's going to the hospital again?" My mom went to the hospital a lot. Sometimes she would have complications from her cancer or chemotherapy or radiation, and one time while she was in the hospital, she had one lung removed. I hated it when she had to stay there because a lot of the time I slept with my mom; Sometimes I would sleep with her in her bed, but when it hurt for her to sleep lying down, she would sleep in her recliner, so I would sleep on the couch next to her. When she was in the hospital, I had to sleep alone.

"No, she's not going to the hospital," Grams replied in a short, somber tone. I don't remember who, but someone told me to go talk to my mom. I walked over to her recliner where she laid slightly tilted back, covered up with her favorite falsa blanket, accompanied by Mr. Buddy, our family cat since before I was born. Mr. Buddy, an all-black cat loved my mom and always slept with her, too. As he got older, he became sick with diabetes and would have to have an insulin shot every day. After we moved to Georgia from California, and my mom became less mobile, she had to teach me how to give Mr. Buddy his insulin shot when she didn't have the energy to move from her chair. Sometimes I would have to catch him and some days he would sit still; I would pull up the fat in the middle of his back, pinch it between my fingers and insert the needle, giving him his 5cc dosage.

"Mom, I have something to tell you," I said nervously. Everyone standing around made me feel uncomfortable. She glanced up at me tiredly, and I whispered down in her ear, "I love you." She smiled and said, "I love you, too." I gave her a kiss on her cheek and minutes later I saw my Aunt Erika move her hand over my mom's eyes, and when her hand lifted from my mom's face, my mom was asleep. I looked around the living room and Grams was crying. My Aunt Jacquelyn and Uncle Brett were hugging; My sister was crying to my Uncle Craig on the back patio. Nothing felt right. I don't remember who, or exactly how, but it was relayed to me in some way that my mom would never wake up. And what seemed like minutes later, a white van that read "Coroner" on the side pulled into our driveway. I kneeled down in the carport next to my mom's white Chevy Beretta and begged, pleaded, and yelled for them not to take her until someone finally carried me off.

Once we got to my Aunt Jacquelyn and Uncle Brett's house, I just laid in his lap and watched the ceiling fan above me go 'round and 'round and 'round. I couldn't move and every now and then I would feel a single tear fall down my cheek and trickle down my neck into a puddle of nothingness just like me. People were talking in the background, but I couldn't hear what they were saying. I was trying to imagine what the next day would be like without my mom; What would it be like to sleep without her? To wake up and never see her again? Who's going to take us to school? Where am I going to live? How am I going to live?

The day after my Mom died, me and my sister were told to stick little circle neon-colored tags onto items in our rooms, the living room, and kitchen. I didn't know it then but when I would be older, I'd wish I had all of those things we were made to sell. Everything except that LFO CD.

Lincoln Park, San Diego

Niños racing on the lawn;

Ice cream truck is circling.

Mischievous giggling soars

over the apartments. The

outsiders do not care for

the 'four corners of death' or

the helicopters flying

every other night. Isn't

there danger in every hood?

Paletero cart bell is ringing.

Tejano music bellows

out from the neighbor's windows.

Graffiti art line alleys

like art galleries

in museums.

Haiku(s) – Part I

When the grass is cut
and the pavement smells of rain
I think of Georgia.

The wind whips at night
violently at my window
the pine trees scatter.

I painted my face
because society said
this is what's beautiful.

It's hands up, don't shoot
Black men are not criminal
because you're racist.

But what is consent
to a man who has never
been reprimanded?

● ● ●

Intrinsic Mother

I didn't understand the gift
of motherhood
until fourteen years after
my mama died.

I wasn't thinking of what motherhood meant
when my mama's thick black hair fell
in chunks onto the cold tile of
my sister's bathroom floor.

To me
it was normal for her to substitute
the soaring volume on the television
for the voice-box
stolen by cancer
to call us to the living room.

I cried to her in her blue laz-e-boy
that I didn't understand my homework
and she cried with me because
I didn't understand that soon
she could no longer help me.

Neither me or mama knew that through her
battle with cancer
she would pass down
intrinsic motherhood.

I would have never been able to stomach
sleeping in my two-door coupe
with my unborn and eight-year-old,
in an airport parking lot,
if I hadn't first seen mama
suffer and live simultaneously.

Mama was
the epitome
of the phrase
'live as if today is your last.'

Mama taught me how to survive
and love
and be a mama
no matter how much it hurt
or how the long welfare lines
gave me time to question
my pride and ability.

Both my pride and ability
intrinsically come from mama –
from motherhood.

I will pass down this gift
as my mama did to me
to my daughter
who will understand
the *beauty* of motherhood.

● ● ●

Walker Ducker Station Road

I look at the time on the microwave and it says 6:48. The train goes by at 7:15, so that gives me enough time to down a shot of Evan Williams, put on my shoes, have Cole put on his shoes, then head out the door. The dirt road is roughly five minutes away. We slip into our '95 Infiniti, careful to ease our legs on to the leather seats that have been baking in the summer Georgia sun. I roll the sun-roof back and Cole fastens his seatbelt in the backseat. We back down the driveway and make a right at the stop sign, traveling 65 through a shaded tunnel of pine trees; for every break in trees, the sunlight finds us and dances across our faces, my hair whipping along my neck.

We reach the muddied dirt road and I let the car coast, careful not to get stuck, as mud lightly splatters the dinged hub caps. We reach the railroad crossing and park along the ditch.

"You got your change, right?"

"Yep!" Cole says eagerly as he unbuckles and plants his shoes into the warm red clay.

We walk up to the tracks and place our change on the rails; A quarter here, a nickel there, and a dime a little farther down. We make our way back to the car and sit on the hood with arms crossed over our bent knees, waiting for the sound of the train.

I lean back on to the windshield and put my arms over my head. I close my eyes and feel the warm breeze caress my arms. The sound of cicadas fade in and out of the distance. In this very moment, I am alive – not in my monotonous nine-to-five routine, not alone in my room riddled with mid-twenties anxiety. No. Here, in this moment, I am aware. I turn toward Cole and watch as he keeps an eye out for the train. I half-smile and admire his dirty blonde hair and tanned skin that's been kissed by the sun in June, and am reminded I am doing something right.

"I think I hear the train," Cole says, interrupting the cicada's harmonies.

I sit up so that I can listen. He's right. Slowly, the train rumbles in our direction. No city train, it passes by slow enough for the conductor to see our familiar faces, smile and nod, as the commotion flattens our now valuable metals.

After the train passed a good enough distance, we jump down from the hood of our hooptie and rush to find our finished products. We scour the graveled space between the rails; I find one quarter on a wooden slate, Cole gathers his from the outskirts. When we're done, we meet by the car and compare our coins. We trade a quarter for a penny, because the penny flattened better. I feel the daunting feeling of night approaching as the breeze turns still and a cool chill settles in. The cicadas are now joined by crickets, and this tells me it's time to go home; Time to prepare dinner, lay out school and work outfits, sweep the kitchen, wrestle in the sheets over the dread of it all.

I glance in the rearview mirror to see the moon

follow us all the way home. I make a left at the stop sign,

traveling through the tunnel of pine trees; For every break

in trees, the light from the dimly lit moon illuminates our

faces.

● ● ●

Practical Magic

Tonight I watched *Practical Magic* for the first time in years;
It reminded me why I both hate and love to watch it.
A story of two sisters, both without their mother –
Inseparable.
I must be Nicole Kidman and you Sandra Bullock.
While I watched, I thought of North Georgia and our new
life away from California;
It was a new life, an end of another life.
The nostalgia was overwhelming and my loneliness
became apparent.
In the movie
When one sister misses the other, the other can sense it.
Do you ever sense my sadness from your absence?
Do we see the same moon?
Would you come if I called?
Impossible.
For I have cried Pacific Ocean tears for you, yet the moon
still pulls the tide in
And I cry to send it back out.
We do not see the same moon.
You have separated me from you.
Our movie has no happy ending.
Only practical magic could bring you back.

Just the Two of Us

Like clockwork, every Saturday at lunch time, Cameron's best friend, Emmanuel, knocks at our door to call Cameron out to play. This day is no different. Small footsteps race down the hallway until they reach the open doorway to my dimly-lit bedroom.

"Mama, can I go outside to play with Emmanuel?" Cameron asked, out of breath.

"Did you already fold your clothes and put them up?" I questioned rhetorically. "What about all of the toys still on your floor? You know the rules, Cameron, everything has to be done before you can go outside."

His shoulders slumped forward, seemingly befuddled by the answer I give every time his room's a mess. He turned around, let out a sigh and I could feel his eyes rolling into the back of his head as he made his way back down the hall to deliver the bad news to Emmanuel. The front door shut and he walked passed my bedroom without even a side eye in my direction. I tiptoed to his room and looked on as he began to pull clothes from the pile on his bed to fold. He made sure to look pitiful as he did it in hopes that I would give in and halt the torture. But I rarely did. As much as I wanted him to go outside and just only worry about being a kid, I also wanted to teach him independence and self-reliance; I prided myself on this as a single mother.

I walked into his room, carefully stepping over scattered train track and K'nex pieces; Over the years I made it a point to make sure that his room, his own sacred space, was decorated with things that most eight to nine-year-old boys were into. On the wall over his bed hangs a Justin Bieber poster that came with the CD he got for Christmas last year. That CD sits in the hand-me-down boombox atop his blue worn baseball-themed dresser. Just next to that is a stack of letters from his Dad. Some days I will walk past his bedroom to see him sitting on his bed reading them. I sit down next to the pile of laundry and attempt to finalize details of his upcoming birthday party.

"So, do you still want to have your party at the skating rink or has it changed again?"

"Yeah. Emmanuel's mom said he could go."

"Well, do you want to invite anyone else? Maybe some other kids from class?"

"No, not really."

A long pause ensued as I thought of anything else I could ask in regards to planning a birthday party for two at a skating rink. Then, Cameron took a deep breath and asked about his Dad.

"Do you think my Dad will be able to come this time?"

I could tell he was nervous about asking but hopeful of the answer I would give. He doesn't know that his father is in prison. He just thinks that his dad lives somewhere else and is always unable to come to any of his events. His dad wasn't there for his preschool graduation or the end-of-the-year field day at his elementary school last year and his dad never shows up to any of his award assemblies where he is often honored for perfect attendance or honor roll.

"I'm sorry, baby. He's not going to be able to come this year. I know you miss him, but there's nothing I can do."

Cameron sighed, "But why can't you tell him to come? Doesn't he want to come? What if I asked him in a letter?"

This is always the hard part. Not only do I have to lie to him, but I have to break his heart at the same time. Somehow, even though I'm not the one incarcerated, I'm the bad guy who always gives the bad news. The one that always has to say, "No." His father wants to be the one to tell him, but I suppose he either still hasn't found the heart or is ashamed – maybe both.

"I'm sure he would love to come, Cameron. But he wouldn't be able to get here from where he lives. I could see if your Poppy would want to come. How about that?"

Poppy is Cameron's favorite, fun grandpa, who is ironically my strict, marine-veteran father.

"I guess," he mumbled back. "I just wish I was like the other kids at school and had both my parents. Emmanuel's dad goes to everything. Why can't he just move back?" He looked down as he asked, rubbing his clammy palms up and down against his pants leg.

"I wish it were that easy, Cam. But, as soon as you get done with your clothes, just leave them folded on your bed and I'll put them in the drawers for you. Once you finish, pick up the toys from the floor and you can go down to Emmanuel's." I kissed him on the forehead and returned to my room to avoid getting emotional.

Falling back on to the bed, I lay against the pillows and close my eyes, imagining myself as an eight-year-old boy without a father – what it must feel like to take on so much at a young age, to be the man of the house, to feel like something is missing. Every evening I watch him tie the kitchen trash bag and head toward the back door to take out the trash, and while I'm proud to be raising the young man he is becoming, I can't help but think of how it would be different had his father not taken the path he did. Am I doing this single mother thing right?

I rummage through the lower cabinet beside the stove to find the large skillet I inherited from my Papa's estate sale, where I actually inherited a lot of my dishes and furniture that occupy mine and Cameron's small two-bedroom home. Once the chicken's sautéed a bit, I put it in the oven and add the pasta to the boiling water. The microwave clock reads 4:52, which means Cameron should be in any minute. Every day that he is outside playing, he knows to be in by 5:00pm. When he comes in, we eat, shower, and wind down for the next work and or school day. I pull the chicken out of the oven, drain the pasta, and fix Cameron's plate.

His food sits on his Toy Story placemat for twenty minutes before I realize it's almost half-past 5. He's not out in the backyard or playing basketball in the driveway. He's not on the futon watching T.V. or in the bathroom washing up. I open up the front door and step onto the welcome mat in my socks, pulling my sweater together and listen for him and Emmanuel. Something's not right; There's no sound of a basketball bouncing or ricocheting off the backboard of the goal set up in the cul-de-sac. I don't hear any boys yelling, "tag!" or laughing hysterically while Emmanuel's rusty trampoline springs creak– only cicada bugs and crickets fill the evening air. I walk back to my bedroom to find my shoes and zip up my sweater. I check the magnolia tree out back where he's known to hide when he's mad at me, but he's not there either. I grab my keys and walk down to Emmanuel's house. My feet glide along the pavement faster with each step. Patricia, Emmanuel's mom, pulls open the door.

"Hey, is Cameron still over here?"

"No... he hasn't been over at all today, I don't think. I got home around three; let me go ask E. Come on in!" Patricia opened the screen door and I stepped in and waited, listening for Cameron's voice. Patricia came out of the hallway. "No ma'am. Emmanuel said Cameron told him he couldn't come out until he finished his chores, but he never did come down to get Emmanuel. Is everything okay?"

"Well, Cameron left out earlier this afternoon after he finished folding his clothes and I assumed he was coming down here. I'm going to go back home and double check to make sure he's not messin' with me or hiding out back somewhere."

"Okay, well, let me know!"

I feel my body getting hot and cold at the same time, my stomach drops over and over as I jog back to the house to check every square inch of the yard. The side of the house near the air conditioning unit is clear; same with the magnolia tree I double-checked in the back. I enter through the french doors into the kitchen and check the laundry room, but it's empty. His room is clean, laundry is folded neatly on top of his bed still. I then realize I hadn't put up his laundry, and if I had I would have noticed his backpack gone. I look around his room to see what else is missing; his favorite Toy Story blanket is gone as well as some clothes from the pile on his bed. *He ran away?*

"911, what is your emergency?" A monotone voice asks over the receiver of my cell phone.

"I think my son's run away! He left out earlier to play with his friend down the street, but didn't come home at the normal time he comes home every evening. I went down to his friend's house and he wasn't there; I've checked everywhere at our home inside and out and he's gone!"

"Ma'am are you sure there's nowhere else he could be? Does he have any other friends in the neighborhood?"

"No, Emmanuel is the only boy he plays with outside of school. Listen, I wouldn't have called unless it was an absolute emergency."

"I understand, ma'am, I'm just trying to collect as much information as possible. What makes you think your son has run away? Was there something that happened recently that would cause him to want to leave?"

I glance over at the stack of letters from Cameron's dad on his dresser and remember our conversation from earlier in the day. Maybe he left because of our conversation. Maybe he left because of me. I didn't have the time to think about it, but now I had more of an idea of what may have happened, so I hung up the phone and rushed to grab the keys off the kitchen counter and jolted out the door to find him myself.

Driving slow, I take the same route we take every day to work and school. I peer onto the sidewalks, the benches at the bus stops, and at kids pulling their scooters across crosswalks. He knows this route like the back of his hand, surely he wouldn't go any other way. While driving, I try to put myself in his shoes once again, this time trying to figure out where an eight-year-old boy would want to go; what could possibly be going through his mind? Just as I reach the intersection next to his school, my phone starts buzzing. I glance down at it sitting in the cupholder and see the screen says Police Department. I pull over into the Harvey's Grocery parking lot and answer.

"Hello?"

"Yes, may I please speak to Ms. Rogers?" A deep-voiced man asks.

"This is she..."

"Hi Ms. Rogers. I believe I have your son, Cameron, here at the station. We found this phone number in his backpack."

"Is he okay?! Please tell me he's okay!"

"Yes ma'am, he's just fine. He stopped by looking for somebody – I can explain more once you get here. We're at the station downtown."

The Chatham County Police Department is across the street from Cameron's school, roughly a fifteen-minute drive from our house. When he began school there, I made it a point to make sure he knew that it was across the street and if there was ever any emergency at school, and

God forbid I wasn't reachable, to walk there for help. I

eased into the Department's parking lot – making sure to

obey the traffic laws, as I didn't need any more trouble –

and hopped out to rush to the front. As soon as I walked

through the sliding doors I see Cameron sitting in the lobby

with his backpack strapped to his back. I quickly head

toward him and wrap my arms tightly around him, covering

his face with all the Mama sugar.

"Baby, are you ok?! I have been so worried about

you!"

"I'm fine mama," Cameron replied softly.

"Ms. Rogers, can I talk to you over here for a

minute?" The deep voiced-man, identified as Captain

Weatherall, called me over to the side of the lobby.

"Hi, Ms. Rogers, it's nice to meet you, my name is

Captain Weatherall. So, here's what happened. Your son

came in here, by himself, with an envelope in hand.

Apparently, he asked Mrs. Cook up here at the front if she

could help him find an address that he was trying to visit.

He told her that this was his father's address and he wanted to know how to get there; he was hoping she could look it up on the computer."

My heart sinks into my shoes and I turn to look at Cameron, sitting alone with disappointment written all over his face. It was almost too unbearable.

"Of course, Mrs. Cook recognized the address on the envelope as the Chatham County Prison and told your son that he would be unable to visit this address. He didn't understand and that's when Mrs. Cook called me up, and then I of course found your number in his backpack and here we are."

"I see," I sighed. This was not how I envisioned this conversation happening at all. "Well, thank y'all so much for being kind, getting in touch with me, and of course, letting me be the one to tell him."

I walked over to Cameron and caressed the back of his light brown hair. "Come on baby, let's go."

Once we get in the car, I inhale and then let out one big exhale. I turn to him and he's looking out the window, holding his chin in his palm.

"Your dad was supposed to be the one to tell you this, but your Dad is in prison, Cameron. That's why you can't visit his address. It's why he won't be able to make it to your party and why he hasn't been able to come to any of your assemblies." He turns and looks at me with confusion. "Your dad found himself in trouble a few years back after doing things he wasn't supposed to do. He admitted to doing those things, and now he has to stay in jail until it's time for him to get out. He won't get out for at least eight more years, baby."

"Eight more years?" He asked with eyebrows raised.

"Eight more years," I confirmed. "I know that you want us all to be together and to be a family like your other friends at school are. I know that you feel left out when other fathers show up for events at school – and to birthday parties – but me and you, we *are* a family. We're just a unique family."

"I guess," he muttered under his breath. I could tell he had a lot to process and it would take a lot more than a conversation in the car for me to make it all make sense. In reality, there would be questions that only his father could answer for him.

I put my hands under his chin and lift his face to turn toward mine. "Look at me. I love you and I'm always going to be here for you no matter what. If you ever have any questions, if you're ever feeling sad, mad, or confused, you can always talk to me about it, ok? We're a team; You and me against the world."

He half smiled and shook his head. I turned the key in the ignition and we pulled our seatbelts across our bodies, both exhausted.

"I do have one question," he said.

"What's that?"

"Can you take out the trash tonight?"

I smiled and chuckled a bit, "Yes Cameron. I can take out the trash tonight."

● ● ●

12/17/14 Today I am grateful for:

- The sunrise
- My 3 beautiful children
- The roof over our head
- Running water
- The food on our table
- My partner in life
- The clothes on our back
- All of my family
- My many memories
- Conversation
- Aiyana's contagious smile
- Sunny California weather
- Transportation
- Mine & my family's health
- The ability to communicate
- Cole's blossoming relationship with his father.
- Old & new friends
- Music
- The sunset
- God
- Life

He

I peep him

in his Brown skin.

It glistens

like the gold flakes

that lie in the sand

beneath the sparkling Pacific Ocean.

His eyes are

bright like the sun;

Like when it peaks through

the spanish moss swaying from an oak tree.

His smile is wide

like my hips

that bore two of the seeds

he planted in me.

He...

I peep him in his
brown skin.
It glistens
Like the gold flakes
that lie in the sand
beneath the Pacific Ocean.

His eyes are bright
Like the sun
Like when it peaks through
the ~~sco~~ spanish moss
hanging from a willow tree.

His smile is wide
Like my hips
that have
bore? ~~birthed~~ two of the
seeds
he planted in me.

Skittish

I'm skittish.

     You adopted me

     from a broken home.

          My previous lover

        was abusive,

    so now

I cower

from love.

September 8, 2017

"SKITTISH"

I'm skittish.
You adopted me from a
broken home.
My previous lover was
abusive.
So now I cower from love

Family Matters

Like a joystick

he toggles my feet back and forth –

His curls sprung in every direction,

his diaper heavy with last night's juice.

When this doesn't work,

he must crawl through the obstacle course

of mine and his dad's legs

entangled in the sheets.

Cold, short fingers pry my eyelids upward.

"Mama," he says softly under his milk breath.

I lie still like a possum.

His curls sweep across my face

as he settles down on top of me

to wait it out.

I hear the other wrestling

to get up from under her fleece blanket.

She scales the bed with ease

and joins her brother

in their morning ritual.

Graceless, she clambers over arms and legs,

not caring about who or what she stumbles over.

She yells out, "Dada!"

and rocks his shoulders back and forth,

trying to upheave him from slumber.

He lets out a grizzly bear grunt and

his cubs scramble toward his embrace.

Though still heavy, I lift the weight

from my eyelids to witness love.

The blankets are disheveled;

love's warmth covers me.

Loss... May 2018

When me & your Dada found out that you were in my belly, we were both elated.

I remember looking @ the stick to see a positive symbol & just feeling instant gratitude that I would have the chance to be a Mama to another beautiful being.

The happiness was overwhelming to the point of tears... just the thought of growing with you, feeling you, loving on you; what would you look like? I felt an impatience, almost, @ the thought of having to wait to meet you.

Little did I know I would have to wait longer than I orginally thought.

I loved you for the rest of my life as soon as I found out about you. And although you are no longer housed in my body, you are still in my heart and soul and and I will never forget you. I will always love you, and so will Dada.

I hope you can find peace at sea and in the ocean like I do. Whenever I find myself immersed in the ocean I will think of you and it will connect us again.

I am always with you.

I love you.

Love,
Mama

Edit:

I buried you in a spider plant that I have hanging in the window @ home so that you can still be close to me. I look at the plant and think of you often.

Love you always…
- Mama

When me & your Dada found
out that you were in my belly,
we were both elated.

I remember looking @ the stick to
see a positive symbol & just
feel like feeling instant
gratitude that I would
have the chance to be a
mama to another beautiful
being.

The happiness was overwhelming
to the point of tears... just
the thought of growing with
you, feeling you, loving on
you; what would you look
like? I felt an impatience,
almost, @ the thought of
having to wait to meet you.

Little did I know I would
have to wait longer than I
originally thought.

I loved you for the rest of my
life as soon as I found out
about you. And although you

are no longer housed in
my body, you are still in
my heart and soul and
I will never forget you.
I will always love you and
so will Dada.

I hope you can find peace at
sea and in the ocean like I
do. Whenever I find myself
immersed in the ocean I
will think of you and it
will connect us again.

I am always with you.

I love you. ♡

Love,
Mama

Edit:
I buried you in a spider
plant that I have hanging
in the window @ home so
that you can still be close
to me. I look at the plant
& think of you often. ♡
Love you always... Mama

Haiku(s) Part II

How's it possible
to still love you after all
the things that you did?

How ironic of
you to work on you with her.
I worked too. *alone*

My resilience is
not of this world I am
so otherworldly.

Principles, morals
Integrity in motion
I am a vessel.

We lost our baby
and you planted one in her
I won't recover.

Never Fold

At the first sign

of trouble

you folded.

I can't

relate.

Future Tense

I used to turn myself on

get myself off

and then

turn you

out.

Just the caress of my own hands against my breasts, down

my side to my widening hips and the crease that lies in

between, would have my legs gliding up and down the

sheets.

The flavor that came out was sweet in my mouth and in

yours, too; I would let you taste.

These moments turned into children, into family, into busy

schedules, and into distractions.

After my third child, my body was so unfamiliar. The

surgery was painful, both emotionally and physically.There

was less time than before for myself and I transformed. I

didn't turn myself on anymore. There was no caressing –

only a desire to get some sort of fulfillment from

somewhere. I wanted to cum to forget and to distract

myself. I was so defeated, both emotionally and physically.

The miscarriage...

If I don't turn myself on, I can not turn you on. I gotta love

this. I'm learning to love this.

Again.

Motherhood

Motherhood is subjective;
There is no mother
that is the same
as another.

Motherhood

Motherhood is subjective. There is no mother that is the same as another.

Pannies

Slip them off, no –

pull them to the side.

They are only in the way

of your hand against

my lips.

It's too wet, anyway,

they will only get drenched.

So just,

pull them to the side

and

pay them no mind,

as your touch

slip and slides,

sending chills up my spine.

Yes –

just like that.

Your breath on my neck

is my favorite

morning sex.

Personifcation

I am emotion personified:

       flesh and fury.

● ● ●

Litany Lament

I'm afraid this callus

will never soften.

It will only get

harder, breaking open

from more contact.

It is, anyway, only an

addendum to the scars

left from the afterbirth;

The tension of muscle memory.

It is suffocating;

a euphemisim for

torment.

Love is Unconditional

The women who stay

are so often deemed

as   weak

even though

it would be easier

to   flee

the strength lies in

understanding

compassion

even   we

you know

and

I know

what this love

could   be

find me in

your darkest moments

and

I will set

you   free

when I say

I love you

I mean

u n c o n d i t i o n a l l y.

Pressure

They say that
'pressure makes diamonds'
So I guess
I'm a diamond in the rough –

In the rough part
of the neighborhood
and always in the
rough part of my life.

'They' don't know that
as a mother, I am the
most beautifully cut
diamond
with immaculate clarity.

My babies don't see me as
a diamond in the rough,
nor do they see
the pressure
that makes me
shine.

PRESSURE

5/17/20

They say that
"pressure makes diamonds"
so
I guess
I'm a diamond in the rough —

in the rough part
of
the neighborhood
and
always
in the
rough part of my life.

"They" don't know that as
a mother
I am
the most beautifully-
cut diamond
with immaculate
clarity.

My babies don't see me as
a diamond in the rough
nor
do they see the
pressure
that makes me
shine.

About the Author

Brooke, who goes by Alex, was born in Beaufort, South Carolina and raised in both Oceano, California and Albany, Georgia. At an early age, she developed a passion for writing stories, studying musical lyrics, and journaling through grief after losing her mother at the age of eleven. Today, she holds an Associate of Arts in English and is a mother of three. *Whether You Like It or Not* is Alex's first published book.

Follow Alex on social media:

Instagram
Personal: @b.alexandriaa
Creative: @maryroxanne.etc

● ● ●

www.ingramcontent.com/pod-product-compliance
Lightning Source LLC
Chambersburg PA
CBHW071241090426
42736CB00014B/3172